Preparing the Wedding Homily

A Guide for Preachers and Couples

Paul Turner

Resource Publications, Inc.
San Jose, California

Also in the Celebrating the Sacraments series:
Eucharist! by Susan S. Jorgensen and *Meaningful First Communion Liturgies* by
Nick Wagner

Reprint Department
Resource Publications, Inc.
160 E. Virginia #290
San Jose, California 95112-5876
(408) 286-8505 voice
(408) 287-8748 fax

Library of Congress Cataloging-in-Publication Data
Turner, Paul, 1953-
    Preparing the wedding homily : a guide for preachers and couples /
        Paul Turner.
        p. cm. — (Celebrating the sacraments series)
    ISBN 0-89390-569-0
        1. Wedding sermons. 2. Marriage—Sermons. 3. Catholic Church—Sermons.
        I. Title. II. Series.

    BV4278 .T87 2003
    251'.1—dc21

                                                            2002037039

Printed in the United States of America
03 04 05 06 07 | 5 4 3 2 1

Editor: Nick Wagner
Production staff: Romina Saha, Nelson Estarija, Tiffany Colonna, Judy Clark

IOANNI ET REBECCÆ TVRNER

QVI VIVVNT QVOD CREDVNT

SIGNVM VTI AMORIS ET FIDELITATIS

ECCLESIÆ IN DOMO

Contents

Acknowledgments

I wish to thank

Nick Wagner, who asked,

Brian Torrey, who wondered,

Dan Harris, who taught,

The engaged, who shared,

God, who loves.

P.T.

Excerpts from the Lectionary for Mass copyright © 1970, 1986, 1992, 1998, 2001 Confraternity of Christian Doctrine, Inc., Washington, D.C. All rights reserved. No part of this work may be reproduced or transmitted in any form or by any means, electronic or mechanical, including photocopying, recording, or by any information storage and retrieval system, without permission in writing from the copyright owner.
   The English translation of the General Introduction, some Psalm responses, some Alleluia and Gospel verses, and the Lenten Gospel Acclamations, some Summaries, and the Titles and Conclusion of the Readings, from the Lectionary for Mass © 1968, 1981, 1997, International Committee on English in the Liturgy, Inc., Washington, D.C. All rights reserved.

Published with the approval of the Committee on the Liturgy,United States Conference of Catholic Bishops.

The English translation of the Psalm Responses from Lectionary for Mass © 1997, 1981, 1969, International Committee on English in the Liturgy, Inc. (ICEL); excerpts from the English translation of the Rite of Marriage © 1969, ICEL. All rights reserved.

Introduction

The wedding homily interprets God's word for the couple and the community. The homily is one element of a complex ceremony involving many words, gestures, music, decorations, ministers, families, friends, and fashions. The success of the ceremony does not rest on the homily. But with careful preparation, the preacher can shed light on the meaning of this event for the couple, the community, and the world.

Whether you are the preacher, the bride, or the groom, this book intends to help you prepare for the wedding homily. It works best if all three of you work on it together.

First you'll remember what a homily is. Then you'll explore more about who the couple is. You will also think about the family and friends who will attend the wedding. Finally, you'll learn what the Scriptures are. The responsibility then falls to the preacher to deliver the results. With all this preparation, those results should be rewarding.

The attentive preacher and couple will enter this task with some apprehension. This book will invite you into some very personal discussions. The couple will share a lot about their lives. The preacher will share experience about God. Together you will approach this wedding as a special spiritual moment. In the homily, you can share the fruits of your conversation with all who attend the ceremony to offer their friendship and to witness the love of Christ and the couple.

Preparing the wedding homily is different from preparing most other homilies. On a typical Sunday, the preacher takes the Scriptures that appear in the lectionary for the day and then talks about their application. At a wedding, however, the readings come from a pool of options. You can choose from among them the readings that best fit the occasion. Preparing the wedding homily also includes selecting the wedding Scriptures.

On Sundays, the preacher studies the assigned Scriptures to determine the homily's theme. But at weddings, you may first discuss themes and then search for apt scriptures. That makes this preaching unique.

This book will help you reflect on the lives of the bride and groom of this unique wedding and listen for what the Spirit is prompting the preacher to say to the people gathered for its celebration.

May God guide you through this task. May you discover God's love in new ways.

The Homily

In the homily, the preacher unveils the mysteries of the faith and proclaims the guiding principles of the Christian life (*Constitution on the Sacred Liturgy* 52). The homily generally builds on texts from the sacred Scriptures and the flow of the liturgical seasons, but it may also draw from other texts of the Mass. It addresses the needs of the listeners (*Inter Oecumenici* 54), enabling them to participate in the whole celebration with faith (*Fulfilled in Your Hearing* III).

The preacher has a large responsibility. A good homilist will help people enter the mystery of God, making them more aware of God's presence in their lives. Therefore, a dutiful preacher will spend time in prayer to prepare for this thoroughly spiritual task.

The people who listen to the homily come with their own experience and faith. They gather for common worship, yet each one hears the word of God in a unique way. As a body, they represent the church gathered in prayer, open to God's Word, ready to respond.

This is where the homily is heading. It will lead people from faith to response. It will address them as a community of believers and challenge them to action in answer to the proclaimed word.

In sum, a homily is a message based on the Scriptures, liturgical texts, or the nature of the celebration addressed to an assembled community of believers. It invites them into deeper appreciation of the mystery of God and challenges them to respond to God's word.

At a wedding, the homily has an added purpose. The preacher is encouraged to address the principles of the faith pertaining to marriage (*Rite of Marriage* 1–5). The homily covers "the mystery of Christian marriage, the dignity of wedded love, the grace of the sacrament and the responsibilities of married people, keeping in mind the circumstances of this particular marriage" (22).

Obviously, all of that is too much to put into one homily. Some of these points will be treated in the couple's preparation for marriage. The homily will provide an opportunity to focus on some aspect of this marriage in a message that will touch the hearts of the couple and the assembly of their family and friends.

Some of those attending the wedding may have little or no faith. They may have come more to support the bride and groom than to pray for them. They, too, will hear the word of God and react to it according to their own experience. The wedding homily, perhaps more than the Sunday homily, will reveal the mystery of God to some who have not yet perceived it.

The Couple

Every couple is unique. The engaged partners yearning for Christian
marriage come with their own stories of faith, both as individuals and
as a couple. Preparation for marriage invites the partners to examine
their spiritual journeys. They will search their memories to discern how
the hand of God has guided them to this point in their lives.

Here are some questions to help the couple discuss with the
preacher how God has been active in their lives. Some questions ask
about their individual lives. Others ask about their lives as a couple.
The preacher may keep the bride and groom together for these
questions, making sure that each has a chance to respond fully.

Questions for the Bride and Groom Individually

What are your principle religious beliefs? Do you believe in God? Do
you believe that Jesus is the Son of God? Do you believe in eternal
life? What else do you believe?

What do you think about the Catholic Church? Is it a source of pride
or embarrassment? Why?

What people have influenced your faith and beliefs?

Do you pray on your own? How and when do you pray? Do you
worship on Sundays with your church?

Did you ever pray that God would help you find a marriage partner?
What kind of person did you pray for? Do you believe that God
brought you together?

How do your beliefs influence your actions? Give an example of
something you did or avoided because you believed it was right or
wrong in the eyes of God.

What religious experiences have you had in your life? Give one
example of how God was with you when you were younger. Has
your relationship with God changed since then?

Questions for the Couple Together

How did you meet? Has God been a part of your relationship? In
what ways?

What religious activities have you done together as a couple? Have you prayed together? Have you learned about faith together? Have you served others together? In what ways?

— How did the marriage proposal happen? (Was it in any way a spiritual experience?)

Do you believe that God has something in mind for you by giving you this partner for life?

Why would you like a church wedding? Is a church wedding important to your family and friends? Is it important to you? What does a church wedding say about your relationship with God? What does it say about your relationship to the people who worship there?

— What would you like your family and friends to remember about your wedding ceremony?

What message about God would you like them to hear?

— What do you hope to experience in your wedding ceremony?

The Assembly

The community that assembles to celebrate a wedding is always unique. These people come together for this one event; normally, very few of them worship together regularly in the church where the wedding takes place. Many of them will know each other as family and friends. Some, however, will be strangers to everyone but the bride and groom.

When preparing the wedding homily, consider who will be there to hear it.

Which family members will attend this wedding?
Who will be in the wedding party?
What other close friends will attend?
What other groups will be represented? Co-workers? People from church? People who belong to the same clubs or organizations as the bride or groom? People who share their goals and interests?
Who will not be able to attend? Why not? How do the bride and groom feel about that?
What do the people who will attend this wedding believe in? What do they hope for? What have they experienced of love?

Developing Themes

Now the couple and the preacher can address some questions together. These will develop some potential themes for the wedding homily.

What have we already learned about God in this engagement?
What does this wedding celebrate?
What message in the homily would affirm what the couple has experienced about God?
What message in the homily would challenge the couple?
What message would affirm what the assembly has experienced about God through this couple?
What message would challenge the assembly?
What are some themes that this homily could proclaim?

The Wedding Lectionary

A lectionary is a collection of Scripture passages arranged for daily, seasonal, and special usage at church. In the Roman Catholic Church, the lectionary offers a wide variety of readings that may be used in a wedding ceremony.

These readings fall into groups: Old Testament passages, New Testament passages (other than the Gospels), responsorial psalms, and Gospel passages. The next chapter contains all of these readings. One of the Scriptures you choose must make a direct reference to marriage. These are marked with an asterisk.

The couple and the preacher will need to know the date of the ceremony and whether or not the wedding will include Mass. Both these elements affect the choice of readings.

When both the bride and groom are Catholic, the wedding normally includes Mass. If one is unbaptized, it does not. If both are baptized but only one is Catholic, the assumption is that the wedding will not include Mass, but it may if desired.

In the Catholic Church, the rules governing the usage of the wedding lectionary are quite complicated. The one constant factor is that the last reading will come from the Gospels.

1. If the wedding does not include a Mass, choose a Gospel from the wedding lectionary, determine how many other readings you would like people to hear before it, and choose a responsorial psalm to follow the first reading.

    a. If you want two readings before the Gospel, as you typically hear each Sunday at church, the choice of readings depends on the season of the year.

        i. If your wedding takes place during the Easter season (between Easter Sunday and Pentecost Sunday), the first reading should come from the Book of Revelation and the second from another New Testament book apart from the Gospels.

      ii. If your wedding takes place at any other time, select the first reading from the Old Testament and the second from the New Testament, but not from the Gospels.

    b. If you want only one reading before the Gospel, the choice also depends on the season of the year.

      i. If your wedding takes place during the Easter season, your first reading should come from the New Testament but not from the Gospels.

      ii. If your wedding takes place at any other time, select one reading from either the Old Testament or the New Testament but not from the Gospels.

2. If the wedding does include a Mass, determine which Mass texts may be used.

    a. If the wedding occurs on any of the most important days of the church year, you may choose only one reading from the wedding lectionary to replace one of the readings already assigned for that day. Be sure to choose your reading from the same category as the one you are replacing. For example, choose a Gospel to replace a Gospel. A wedding Mass on the evening before a Sunday or holyday follows the rules for the Sunday or holyday it immediately precedes. If the wedding takes place on any of the following days, use the lectionary for that day and substitute any one reading with a reading from the wedding lectionary:

      i. During the Easter Triduum (from Holy Thursday night through Easter Sunday night) (*Note:* Weddings are not to be celebrated on Good Friday or Holy Saturday.)

      ii. The solemnities of Christmas (December 25), Epiphany (the Sunday occurring between January 2 and 8 inclusive in the United States; January 6 in many other countries), Ascension (either Thursday of the sixth week of Easter or the Seventh Sunday of Easter, depending on where you live in the world), or Pentecost

      iii. Sundays of Advent, Lent, or the Easter season

      iv. Ash Wednesday

      v. Weekdays of holy week or days within the octave of Easter

      vi. Solemnities of the Holy Trinity (the Sunday after Pentecost), of the Body and Blood of Christ (the Sunday after Holy Trinity in the United States, but the Thursday after Holy Trinity in many other countries), of the Sacred Heart (the second Friday after Trinity Sunday), or of Christ the King (last Sunday in Ordinary Time)

vii. Solemnities of Mary the Mother of God (January 1), the Annunciation (March 25), the Assumption (August 15), or the Immaculate Conception (December 8)

viii. Solemnities of John the Baptist (June 24), Peter and Paul (June 29), or All Saints (November 1)

ix. All Souls (November 2)

x. Solemnity of the principal patron of your city or state; of the dedication of your church and its anniversary; of the title of your church; or of the title, founder or principal patron of the religious order or congregation associated with your church.

b. If the wedding Mass takes place on any other day—including a Saturday evening during Ordinary Time—choose a Gospel from the wedding lectionary, determine how many other readings you would like people to hear before it, and choose a responsorial psalm to follow the first reading.

i. If you want two readings before the Gospel, as you typically hear each Sunday at church, the choice of readings depends on the season of the year.

1. If your wedding takes place during the Easter season (between Easter Sunday and Pentecost Sunday) on a day not listed under 2a above, the first reading should come from the Book of Revelation, and the second comes from another New Testament book apart from the Gospels.

2. If your wedding takes place at any other time on a day not listed above, select the first reading from the Old Testament and the second from the New Testament but not from the Gospels.

ii. If you want only one reading before the Gospel, the choice also depends on the season of the year.

1. If your wedding takes place during the Easter season on a day not listed under 2a above, your first reading should come from the New Testament but not from the Gospels.

2. If your wedding takes place at any other time on a day not listed above, select one reading from either the Old Testament or the New Testament but not from the Gospels.

Yes, the rules are complicated.

You will always have the option of choosing at least one Scripture text. On most days you may choose up to three.

If your wedding takes place during Mass on one of the church's most important days (those listed in 2a above), consider these questions first:

What is the nature of the special day the entire church celebrates today?

What is its significance for the church around the world?

What is its significance in the lives of the couple?

How do the spiritual lives of the couple relate to this special day in the church?

Why has the church selected these Scripture readings to celebrate this special day?

What special message might unite the church's day and the couple's day?

The wedding lectionary contains many beautiful passages from the Bible, some more familiar than others. They all deserve your prayer and attention. At the wedding, use the fourth volume of the lectionary (801–805). Each passage appears below with a short commentary. The commentary should help you understand why each passage might be appropriate for your wedding.

Think again about your conversations. How has God entered your life as a couple? What message do you want people to hear at this wedding? Then decide which readings best express the mystery of God's love to be revealed in this marriage.

The Readings

Old Testament Readings

1. * Genesis 1:26–28,31a

Then God said:
  "Let us make man in our image, after our likeness.
Let them have dominion over the fish of the sea,
    the birds of the air, and the cattle,
    and over all the wild animals
    and all the creatures that crawl on the ground."

God created man in his image;
    in the image of God he created him;
    male and female he created them.

God blessed them, saying:
    "Be fertile and multiply;
    fill the earth and subdue it.
Have dominion over the fish of the sea, the birds of the air,
    and all the living things that move on the earth."
God looked at everything he had made, and he found it very good.

God created male and female human beings and commanded them to continue the work of creation through their children.

On the other days of creation, God looked around and pronounced everything good. On this last day, God looked at all creation including humans and pronounced it very good.

No one knows exactly how the earth was made. Some people believe it happened just the way the Bible says. Others accept the conclusions of geologists and astronomers who prove that the universe is much older. Our faith tells us that however and whenever the earth was made, God made it. The Catholic Church does not insist on a literal interpretation of this passage.

We do insist on the underlying truth of this passage. God created everything. Human beings—male and female—are created in God's own image and likeness. Through our affinity with God's divinity we also share an obligation with God's occupation. We create.

God commands us to create and also to rule. God asks humans to govern the resources of the world, whether they are in the sea, in the air, or on the ground.

When we hear this passage at a wedding, it especially reminds the couple of their responsibility as parents. God has already given them a share in humanity. Now they will accept the special responsibility that comes with being human: raising a family.

> This reading makes a good choice for a couple looking forward to the joys and challenges of parenting. It is also good for the couple in tune with the spiritual side of being human. This passage affirms the bride and groom who have experienced God working through them to touch others.

2. * Genesis 2:18-24

The LORD God said: "It is not good for the man to be alone.
I will make a suitable partner for him."
So the LORD God formed out of the ground
    various wild animals and various birds of the air,
    and he brought them to the man to see what he would call them;
    whatever the man called each of them would be its name.
The man gave names to all the cattle,
    all the birds of the air, and all wild animals;
    but none proved to be the suitable partner for the man.

So the LORD God cast a deep sleep on the man,
    and while he was asleep,
    he took out one of his ribs and closed up its place with flesh.
The LORD God then built up into a woman the rib
    that he had taken from the man.
When he brought her to the man, the man said:

    "This one, at last, is bone of my bones
        and flesh of my flesh;
    This one shall be called 'woman,'

for out of 'her man' this one has been taken."

That is why a man leaves his father and mother
and clings to his wife,
and the two of them become one body.

In this story, God creates woman to be a suitable partner for man.

The first two chapters of Genesis give two different accounts of creation. In the first, God creates animals first and then human beings. In this account, God has created a human being and then creates animals as potential partners for the human. None of them suffices. So God puts the human to sleep, pulls a rib out of this creature, and fashions it into a woman. She becomes a suitable partner for the man. The man calls her "bone of my bones and flesh of my flesh."

The writer says that man and woman were created to be together. The reason someone leaves parents and takes a partner is so the two of them can become one.

At a wedding this passage helps us reflect on the purpose of being human. The close company that married partners enjoy expresses not just the thrill of love, but also the importance of love. Love pulls us out of our selfishness. We feel more alive and more human when we love. Because we are.

> This passage is especially appropriate for those who believe God created them for the love they are giving their partner and who feel incomplete without their partner.

3.* Genesis 24:48–51,58–67

The servant of Abraham said to Laban:
"I bowed down in worship to the LORD,
blessing the LORD, the God of my master Abraham,
who had led me on the right road
to obtain the daughter of my master's kinsman for his son.
If, therefore, you have in mind to show true loyalty to my master,
let me know;
but if not, let me know that, too.
I can then proceed accordingly."

Laban and his household said in reply:
  "This thing comes from the LORD;
  we can say nothing to you either for or against it.
Here is Rebekah, ready for you;
  take her with you,
  that she may become the wife of your master's son,
  as the LORD has said."

So they called Rebekah and asked her,
  "Do you wish to go with this man?"
She answered, "I do."
At this they allowed their sister Rebekah and her nurse to take leave,
  along with Abraham's servant and his men.
Invoking a blessing on Rebekah, they said:

  "Sister, may you grow
    into thousands of myriads;
  And may your descendants gain possession
    of the gates of their enemies!"

Then Rebekah and her maids started out;
  they mounted their camels and followed the man.
So the servant took Rebekah and went on his way.

Meanwhile Isaac had gone from Beer-lahai-roi
  and was living in the region of the Negeb.
One day toward evening he went out ... in the field,
  and as he looked around, he noticed that camels were
    approaching.
Rebekah, too, was looking about, and when she saw him,
  she alighted from her camel and asked the servant,
  "Who is the man out there, walking through the fields toward
    us?"
"That is my master," replied the servant.
Then she covered herself with her veil.

The servant recounted to Isaac all the things he had done.
Then Isaac took Rebekah into his tent;
  he married her, and thus she became his wife.
In his love for her Isaac found solace
  after the death of his mother Sarah.

Rebekah becomes the wife of Isaac. He loves her and finds comfort after the recent death of his mother.

This story is included in the wedding lectionary because it relates how Rebekah and Isaac become wife and husband. But the betrothal is unlike anything people expect today.

Abraham has just lost his wife Sarah at the age of 127. In his extreme old age, 136, he decides it is time to find a wife for their son Isaac, who is 36. Obviously, the birth of Isaac had been phenomenal even by biblical standards. Isaac does not try to find his own bride. Abraham supervises the search.

Abraham, living in Canaan, sends his servant back to his homeland to find Isaac a wife from his own nationality. The servant sets out with an impressive display of camels and treasures and goes to Aramnaharaim. There he prays that God would send the future bride of Isaac—whoever she might be—to the well with a jar. The servant plans to ask her for a drink, and suggests to God that if the woman offers to give the camels a drink also, he will know that she is the one God has chosen for Isaac. The conversation happens as the servant had prayed that it would. He gives a nose ring to the woman, Rebekah, and adorns her wrists in bracelets. She takes the servant to her father and brother, and the servant asks them if he can bring Rebekah back to Isaac. After some further conversation, they all agree. The family sends Rebekah off with prayers that her children will be many and powerful.

When Rebekah and the servant return to Abraham's camp, they see Isaac coming toward them. Rebekah covers herself and approaches her betrothed. Isaac takes her into his tent, and they become husband and wife. He loves her. This relieves some of the anguish he felt over the death of his mother.

Chances are that the couple reading this book got engaged some other way. This kind of courtship is so foreign to those in our modern culture that couples rarely choose this reading for the wedding. Even a preacher would hope that two people will spend more time together than Rebekah and Isaac did before getting married.

But there are reasons why this reading might make a good choice. If the partners have a sense that God led them to each other from the moment they first met, there is some relationship between their story and the one told here. If family members have had an active role in supporting the couple's decision to marry, this story relates as well. If the couple met on a blind date, if a parent died recently, or if one partner went through extraordinary lengths to find the other, it might be fitting to tell this story.

4. * Tobit 7:6–14

Raphael and Tobiah entered the house of Raguel and greeted him.
Raguel sprang up and kissed Tobiah, shedding tears of joy.
But when he heard that Tobit had lost his eyesight,
     he was grieved and wept aloud.
He said to Tobiah:
     "My child, God bless you!
You are the son of a noble and good father.
But what a terrible misfortune
     that such a righteous and charitable man
     should be afflicted with blindness!"
He continued to weep in the arms of his kinsman Tobiah.
His wife Edna also wept for Tobit;
     and even their daughter Sarah began to weep.

Afterward, Raguel slaughtered a ram from the flock
     and gave them a cordial reception.
When they had bathed and reclined to eat,
     Tobiah said to Raphael, "Brother Azariah,
     ask Raguel to let me marry my kinswoman Sarah."
Raguel overheard the words;
     so he said to the boy:
     "Eat and drink and be merry tonight,
     for no man is more entitled to marry my daughter Sarah
     than you, brother.
Besides, not even I have the right to give her to anyone but you,
     because you are my closest relative.
But I will explain the situation to you very frankly.
I have given her in marriage to seven men,
     all of whom were kinsmen of ours,

and all died on the very night they approached her.
But now, son, eat and drink.
I am sure the LORD will look after you both."
Tobiah answered, "I will eat or drink nothing
    until you set aside what belongs to me."

Raguel said to him: "I will do it."
She is yours according to the decree of the Book of Moses.
Your marriage to her has been decided in heaven!
Take your kinswoman
    from now on you are her love,
    and she is your beloved.
She is yours today and ever after.
And tonight, son may the Lord of heaven prosper you both.
May he grant you mercy and peace."
Then Raguel called his daughter Sarah, and she came to him.
He took her by the hand and gave her to Tobiah with the words:
    "Take her according to the law.
According to the decree written in the Book of Moses she is your
        wife.
Take her and bring her back safely to your father.
And may the God of heaven grant both of you peace and prosperity."
He then called her mother and told her to bring a scroll,
    so that he might draw up a marriage contract
    stating that he gave Sarah to Tobiah as his wife
    according to the decree of the Mosaic law.
Her mother brought the scroll,
    and he drew up the contract,
    to which they affixed their seals.

Afterward they began to eat and drink.

Tobiah becomes engaged to Raguel's daughter Sarah.

This story appears in the wedding lectionary because it recounts an
engagement and a wedding. But it is a peculiar story.
    Tobit, an old man, blinded by bird droppings while taking an
outdoor nap, sends his son Tobiah on a mission to accomplish several
things, including a search for a wife of his own nationality. Tobit
unwittingly hires the angel Raphael, disguised as a relative named

Azariah, to guide his son Tobiah on the journey. They set off with the pet dog and arrive at the home of Raguel.

As this reading begins, Raguel greets Tobiah and expresses condolences over the blindness of his father. Raguel's wife Edna and daughter Sarah also weep. They all eat a freshly slaughtered ram. Tobiah asks Raphael / Azariah to ask Raguel for permission to wed Sarah. Raguel overhears and assures Tobiah that Sarah is his. But there is one small problem.

Sarah has been married before. Seven times, in fact. Each husband mysteriously died after making love to her on the wedding night. But if Tobiah wants her, she is all his.

He still wants her. So Raguel gives her to him today and forever and prays that God will guide and prosper them both on their wedding night and grant them mercy and peace. He wishes them peace on their journey back to Tobit.

There are reasons why a couple may not want this reading for their wedding. The engagement in this story is very brief and has more to do with ethnicity and love at first sight than it does with a measured, prayerful search for a soul mate. Sarah's frightening bridal history sounds a weird note as today's couple is beginning what they hope to be a lifetime of bliss.

> But other circumstances might make this reading a good choice. One partner may feel that God served as a guide in finding the other, just as the angel Raphael guided Tobiah to find Sarah. Or if the bride and groom are facing extraordinary odds in their relationship (for example, a disability, a conflict in families, or a history of financial stress), they might find comfort in this story where love, faith, and commitment overcome the evil threatening to keep the couple apart.

5. * Tobit 8:4b–8

> On their wedding night Tobiah arose from bed and said to his wife,
> "Sister, get up. Let us pray and beg our Lord
>   to have mercy on us and to grant us deliverance."
> Sarah got up, and they started to pray
>   and beg that deliverance might be theirs.
> They began with these words:

"Blessed are you, O God of our fathers;
    praised be your name forever and ever.
Let the heavens and all your creation
    praise you forever.
You made Adam and you gave him his wife Eve
    to be his help and support;
    and from these two the human race descended.
You said, 'It is not good for the man to be alone;
    let us make him a partner like himself.'
Now, Lord, you know that I take this wife of mine
    not because of lust,
    but for a noble purpose.
Call down your mercy on me and on her,
    and allow us to live together to a happy old age."

They said together, "Amen, amen."

On his wedding night, in the presence of his bride Sarah, Tobiah offers a prayer to God.

And well he should. Seven men have already married Sarah. All of them died on the wedding night. Tobiah did what any God-fearing man would do under the circumstances. He prayed.

He also burned some fish innards. In the verses preceding this passage Tobiah places the liver and heart of a fish on some burning embers of incense. The odor drives away the demon responsible for the deaths of the previous husbands. The angel Raphael, who had accompanied Tobiah on his journey, follows the demon to the outermost parts of Egypt and binds the evildoer so he cannot return.

This passage is the text of Tobiah's prayer. Although the setting is overly dramatic, the text of the prayer is quite lovely. Tobiah praises the God of his ancestors, the maker of Adam and Eve, from whom the whole human race came. He tells God he takes Sarah not out of lust, but with sincerity, and asks that they both may find mercy and grow old together. This beautiful marriage prayer was probably composed independent from the story, and the writer inserted it here. Excerpted from the story, it helps a couple focus their dependence on God.

This reading might be a good choice for partners experiencing any fears about their future. It will fit the couple whose love goes beyond sexual appetites. It will also feel appropriate for the bride and groom who have already made prayer a part of their lives together.

6. * Proverbs 31:10–13,19–20,30–31

When one finds a worthy wife,
　　her value is far beyond pearls.
Her husband, entrusting his heart to her,
　　has an unfailing prize.
She brings him good, and not evil,
　　all the days of her life.
She obtains wool and flax
　　and makes cloth with skillful hands.
She puts her hands to the distaff,
　　and her fingers ply the spindle.
She reaches out her hands to the poor,
　　and extends her arms to the needy.
Charm is deceptive and beauty fleeting;
　　the woman who fears the LORD is to be praised.
Give her a reward of her labors,
　　and let her works praise her at the city gates.

A praiseworthy wife is more valuable than fine pearls.

The Book of Proverbs is a collection of sayings handed down from one generation to another. It includes this portrait of a praiseworthy wife. By today's cultural standards, the passage may sound sexist, but it has merit.

The passage focuses only on the wife. The only praise the husband receives is having her as a spouse.

This wife brings good, not evil. She obtains wool and flax and spins cloth skillfully. She helps the poor and the needy. She may not have the charm and beauty of some other women, but those traits do not last anyway. The real praise belongs to the woman who fears God.

This snapshot depicts a woman with goodness in her heart, skill in her hands, and generosity in her spirit. Although today's brides usually are not adept at spinning flax, they have other marketable skills. For the bride who is morally upright, talented, and generous with her possessions, and for the groom who knows what a treasure she is, this passage acknowledges the loving God who created all these gifts.

7. Song of Songs 2:8–10,14,16a;8:6–7a

Hark! my lover — here he comes
  springing across the mountains,
  leaping across the hills.
My lover is like a gazelle
  or a young stag.
Here he stands behind our wall,
  gazing through the window,
  peering through the lattices.
My lover speaks; he says to me,
  "Arise, my beloved, my dove, my beautiful one, and come!"

"O my dove in the clefts of the rock,
  in the secret recesses of the cliff,
Let me see you,
  let me hear your voice,
For your voice is sweet,
  and you are lovely."

My lover belongs to me and I to him.
  He says to me:

"Set me as a seal on your heart,
  as a seal on your arm;
For stern as death is love,
  relentless as the nether-world is devotion;
  its flames are a blazing fire.
Deep waters cannot quench love,
  nor floods sweep it away."

Love brings joy and possesses strength.

Song of Songs is a collection of love poetry. The title of this book means something like "The Best Song," and it refers to a song about love. This is the only book in the Bible that never mentions God. It is included in the Bible because love is the identity of God.

This reading is a combination of two passages. The first one relates a conversation between the lovers. Springtime is evident from the references to blossoming flora and playful fauna. Love is evident in the way the lover gazes through the windows (the eyes?) of the beloved. As springtime makes new life appear, so love brings the lover out of hiding. The first part of the reading celebrates a love that breaks forth from hibernation into the joys of companionship.

The second part of the reading comes from a poem later in the book. It celebrates the strength of true love. Love is as stern as death. It resembles a blazing fire. Floods cannot drown it. You cannot buy love, no matter how much you offer.

These poems sing of the happiness of young love and the determination to make it last.

> This reading may be appropriate for a springtime wedding, for a youthful couple, for lovers of nature, or for any two people who have felt the overwhelming power of falling in love.

8. * Sirach 26:1–4,13–16

Blessed the husband of a good wife,
    twice-lengthened are his days;
A worthy wife brings joy to her husband,
    peaceful and full is his life.
A good wife is a generous gift
    bestowed upon him who fears the LORD;
Be he rich or poor, his heart is content,
    and a smile is ever on his face.

A gracious wife delights her husband,
    her thoughtfulness puts flesh on his bones;
A gift from the LORD is her governed speech,
    and her firm virtue is of surpassing worth.
Choicest of blessings is a modest wife,
    priceless her chaste soul.
A holy and decent woman adds grace upon grace;

indeed, no price is worthy of her temperate soul.
Like the sun rising in the LORD's heavens,
    the beauty of a virtuous wife is the radiance of her home.

A good wife adorns her house like the rising sun.

The Book of Sirach is also known as Ecclesiasticus. The Catholic
Church includes it among the books of the Bible, but not every
denomination does. The author, Jesus ben Sira, has collected some
sayings to advance the wisdom of the reader. Among his words to live
by is a song of praise to a good wife.

Jesus ben Sira says the husband of a good wife will live twice longer
than a man without one. If a man has faith in God, he can count on
receiving among his blessings a good spouse. He will be happy
regardless of his finances. A wife's charm delights her husband, and her
attention "puts flesh on his bones." According to Jesus ben Sira, a gift
from God is the wife who does not speak much, is modest and chaste.
She shimmers in a well ordered home like the rising sun in the sky.

This portrait of a wife will offend many of its readers. She is to cook
and keep her mouth shut. Her main virtue is bringing happiness to her
husband.

It is hard to dispute the sexist slant of this passage. In its favor,
however, it praises those who have faith in God, love for their partner,
a spirit of service, reservation in speech, modesty, and chastity. It
admirably affirms the need for service in a relationship, but it would be
nice to see the husband called to the same standards.

> The passage appears in the wedding lectionary because it was
> written with sincere admiration for good wives. It might work if
> the other scriptures balance the portrait of a married relationship.
> Otherwise, it may appear that the purpose of the wedding is for
> the groom to get a good bride.

9. Jeremiah 31:31–32a,33–34a

The days are coming, says the LORD,
    when I will make a new covenant with the house of Israel
    and the house of Judah.
It will not be like the covenant I made with their fathers:
    the day I took them by the hand

to lead them forth from the land of Egypt.
But this is the covenant which I will make
    with the house of Israel after those days, says the LORD.
I will place my law within them, and write it upon their hearts;
    I will be their God, and they shall be my people.
No longer will they have need to teach their friends and relatives
    how to know the LORD.
All, from least to greatest, shall know me, says the LORD.

God makes a new covenant with the house of Israel and the house of Judah.

At first glance this passage has nothing to do with marriage. It has everything to do with the covenant God established with the chosen people.

Much of the first part of the Bible tells how God related to Israel. God established a covenant with these people, and they broke it, and recommitted themselves to it time and again. God always remained faithful, even when the people strayed.

At one point in this big story, enemies routed Israel and carried people away in captivity. In retrospect, prophets told the people the reason for their great social losses was the spiritual loss of their relationship with God. Eventually, the king of Persia allowed the captives to return to their homeland. In this prophecy from Jeremiah we hear God promising to reestablish the covenant with the people.

This new covenant will differ from the old. God wrote the old covenant on stone tablets. This one will be written upon the hearts of the people. All will come to know God by the forgiveness they have received.

The church views marriage as the same kind of covenant God established with Israel. God chose Israel, offered love, and pledged to remain permanently true to the agreement. Even when Israel sinned, God was always ready to take the people back.

Every marriage has its ups and downs. But couples going into Christian marriage enter it with the same commitment that God showed Israel. The love between husband and wife captures the glimmer of the love that God has for us. As a church, we should be able to look to a married couple for an example of that kind of love. We come to know God's love better when we witness the selfless love of husband and wife.

This reading is especially appropriate for the bride and groom aware of God's love for them, even when they have failed to love God back. If partners have experienced separation from each another, from the church, or from God, and if they commit themselves this day to each other, to the community of faith, and to the God who loves them each day, this reading might make a good choice. It also fits the bride and groom who want to emphasize the permanence of their commitment to each other.

New Testament Readings

1. Romans 8:31b–35,37–39

Brothers and sisters:
If God is for us, who can be against us?
He did not spare his own Son
    but handed him over for us all,
    will he not also give us everything else along with him?
Who will bring a charge against God's chosen ones?
It is God who acquits us.
Who will condemn?
It is Christ Jesus who died, rather, was raised,
    who also is at the right hand of God,
    who indeed intercedes for us.
What will separate us from the love of Christ?
Will anguish, or distress, or persecution, or famine,
    or nakedness, or peril, or the sword?

No, in all these things, we conquer overwhelmingly
    through him who loved us.
For I am convinced that neither death, nor life,
    nor angels, nor principalities,
    nor present things, nor future things,
    nor powers, nor height, nor depth,
    nor any other creature will be able to separate us
    from the love of God in Christ Jesus our Lord.

Nothing separates us from the love of God.

The first Christians suffered misunderstanding and persecution. In Paul's letter to the church at Rome, he reassures the believers that God's love overcomes all the obstacles they may face.

If God is on the side of believers, no one has power against them. God already handed over the only-begotten Son, Jesus, to suffer death for us. God will not withhold any other good gift either. Nothing, Paul says, can separate us from God's love: Anguish, distress, persecution, famine, nakedness, peril, and the sword are all powerless against God's love, which comes to us in Christ Jesus.

At a wedding we normally celebrate the love being pledged between bride and groom. But this passage draws us into the love of Christ. Nothing can obstruct God's strong love for us. Even before people give love away, they have received it first from God.

> Choosing this reading will set the couple's love in a broader context. It will affirm the bride and groom who have experienced God's love throughout their lives and especially in this relationship. If they have overcome obstacles to come to this wedding day, this reading will remind them that Christ was with them, loving them, all along. Similarly, if they know the challenges that lie ahead, this reading will comfort them with the assurance that Christ will be there, too. Nothing will separate them from God's love.

2a. Romans 12:1–2,9–18 (long form)

I urge you, brothers and sisters, by the mercies of God,
    to offer your bodies as a living sacrifice,
    holy and pleasing to God, your spiritual worship.
Do not conform yourselves to this age
    but be transformed by the renewal of your mind,
    that you may discern what is the will of God,
    what is good and pleasing and perfect.

Let love be sincere;
    hate what is evil,
    hold on to what is good;
    love one another with mutual affection;

anticipate one another in showing honor.
Do not grow slack in zeal,
    be fervent in spirit,
    serve the Lord,
Rejoice in hope,
    endure in affliction,
    persevere in prayer.
Contribute to the needs of the holy ones,
    exercise hospitality.
Bless those who persecute you,
    bless and do not curse them.
Rejoice with those who rejoice,
    weep with those who weep.
Have the same regard for one another;
    do not be haughty but associate with the lowly;
    do not be wise in your own estimation.
Do not repay anyone evil for evil;
    be concerned for what is noble in the sight of all.
If possible, on your part, live at peace with all.

2b. Romans 12:1–2,9–13 (short form)

I urge you, brothers and sisters, by the mercies of God,
    to offer your bodies as a living sacrifice,
    holy and pleasing to God, your spiritual worship.
Do not conform yourselves to this age
    but be transformed by the renewal of your mind,
    that you may discern what is the will of God,
    what is good and pleasing and perfect.

Let love be sincere;
    hate what is evil,
    hold on to what is good;
    love one another with mutual affection;
    anticipate one another in showing honor.
Do not grow slack in zeal,
    be fervent in spirit,
    serve the Lord,
Rejoice in hope,
    endure in affliction,

persevere in prayer.
Contribute to the needs of the holy ones,
    exercise hospitality.

Love should be sincere.

Paul advises the Roman church how to live as a community. He compares their lives to sacrifices offered to God. People should live in a way that pleases God, as if they were a living sacrifice. They should not conform themselves to this world, but be transformed in such a way that they will know the will of God.

Addressing the whole community, Paul asks that their love be genuine. He asks them to outdo one another in showing affection. Paul urges patience in suffering, perseverance in prayer, contributions to the community, and hospitality to strangers.

Aware that the community faces struggles, Paul asks them to bless their persecutors, be empathic, live in harmony with everyone, and aspire to humility. All this advice is intended to help the community live in peace.

This makes an interesting passage for weddings. Even though the words were originally addressed to an entire church community, these same words can apply to the home, which is the first church. If the couple can live as Paul encourages, there is hope that the broader community can do so as well.

> This passage will express the desires of those who want a home life consistent with their ideals. The bride and groom skilled at conflict resolution and comfortable with differences have the gifts to make their home a Christian community. The words of Paul will help them achieve all that they wish. Their home will help build a strong society.

3. Romans 15:1b–3a,5–7,13

Brothers and sisters:
We ought to put up with the failings of the weak and not to please
    ourselves;
    let each of us please our neighbor for the good,
    for building up.
For Christ did not please himself.

May the God of endurance and encouragement
   grant you to think in harmony with one another,
in keeping with Christ Jesus,
   that with one accord you may with one voice
glorify the God and Father of our Lord Jesus Christ.

Welcome one another, then, as Christ welcomed you,
   for the glory of God.
May the God of hope fill you with all joy and peace in believing,
   so that you may abound in hope by the power of the Holy Spirit.

Welcome one another, as Christ has welcomed you.

Near the end of Paul's Letter to the Romans, he urges the members of the community to express their care for one another. In imitation of Christ, Paul says, we should try to please our neighbor, not ourselves. As Christ has welcomed us, he continues, we should welcome one another.

Paul also prays that God may help the community to live in harmony and fill them with joy and peace, so that the members may have much hope.

Although Paul addresses these words to the entire community, the lectionary adopts this text as a passage for the engaged. The same advice applies. Christ has set an example. One partner should try to please the other, not him or her self.

The advice on welcoming works two ways for the couple. Certainly each partner should welcome the other, but the couple together should also welcome others. As a family, they will form the foundational elements of a Christian community. So the words of Paul apply to them not only as individuals, but as a unit.

> Those who are especially mindful of each other's needs and who accept the challenge of welcoming the broader community into their home and care might request this passage for their wedding. The bride and groom who appreciate that this wedding is not just about them but also about families and the community will find this a beautiful text to ponder.

4. 1 Corinthians 6:13c–15a, 17–20

Brothers and sisters:
The body is not for immorality, but for the Lord,
    and the Lord is for the body;
    God raised the Lord and will also raise us by his power.

Do you not know that your bodies are members of Christ?
Whoever is joined to the Lord becomes one spirit with him.
Avoid immorality.
Every other sin a person commits is outside the body;
    but the immoral person sins against his own body.
Do you not know that your body
    is a temple of the Holy Spirit within you,
    whom you have from God, and that you are not your own?
For you have been purchased at a price.
Therefore glorify God in your body.

Your bodies are temples of the Holy Spirit.

According to Paul's letters, the Corinthian community frequently
sinned against God. His letters to these people span a wide range of
topics, but one specific concern is the moral behavior of the people.

In this passage, Paul stresses the sacredness of the human body and
urges the Corinthians to treat their persons with respect. They are
members of Christ. God has purchased them at a price, Paul notes, and
intends to raise them up. The body is a temple of the Holy Spirit. "You
are not your own," Paul says. So the Corinthians should not let the
body succumb to immoral behavior. The body is destined for
something greater. Believers should glorify God in their bodies. The
body is not for immorality, but for the LORD.

In making this passage part of the wedding lectionary, the church
celebrates the sacredness of the body and joins Paul in his cautions
about the immorality toward which the body is prone. In the context
of the wedding, the sexual overtones of this passage will not be missed.
It reminds the couple that their bodies—soon to be joined in the sexual
union of Christian marriage—are sacred. If their attraction to each other
stops at beauty and sex, they have missed the fuller symbolism of the
human body. The body of the lover is not only an object of pleasure. It
is a member of Christ. It is the dwelling place of the Spirit. It deserves
honor and respect, not self-satisfaction or abuse.

This is the sort of passage you would expect parents or clergy to impose on partners who have neglected the traditional standard of the unique place of sexual relationships within marriage. But it will also be appropriate for the bride and groom who have respectfully refrained from premarital sex, who are committed to sexual fidelity with each other, and who recognize the sacredness of the other person—the presence of God's Spirit within their partner.

5. 1 Corinthians 12:31—13:8a

Brothers and sisters:
Strive eagerly for the greatest spiritual gifts.

But I shall show you a still more excellent way.

If I speak in human and angelic tongues
    but do not have love,
    I am a resounding gong or a clashing cymbal.
And if I have the gift of prophecy
    and comprehend all mysteries and all knowledge;
    if I have all faith so as to move mountains,
    but do not have love, I am nothing.
If I give away everything I own,
    and if I hand my body over so that I may boast
    but do not have love, I gain nothing.

Love is patient, love is kind.
It is not jealous, is not pompous,
    it is not inflated, it is not rude,
    it does not seek its own interests,
    it is not quick-tempered, it does not brood over injury,
        it does not rejoice over wrongdoing
    but rejoices with the truth.
It bears all things, believes all things,
    hopes all things, endures all things.

Love never fails.

Love is the greatest gift of all.

Without a doubt, this is the most popular Scripture passage for Christian weddings. No other chapter in the Bible speaks about love so eloquently. The bride and groom who have experienced love in all its excitement typically find that this passage best summarizes what they have experienced as they approach their wedding day.

But Paul did not write this for a wedding. Engaged couples were probably the farthest thing from his mind. Paul was describing the entire Christian community. In fact, he had in mind a very specific Christian community, the first-century Corinthians.

Earlier in the letter, Paul expressed his concerns that the Corinthians were splintering. Factions of Christians had formed around who was baptized by whom. Paul wanted no part of it. He pleads again and again for unanimity. Near the end of this letter, Paul speaks about the virtue of love. He may have lifted this section from a popular hymn or poem of his day. We are not sure. But it eloquently expresses the kind of love he expected all Christians to have for one another.

The faithful in Corinth have received many spiritual gifts from God. Some teach. Some prophesy. Some interpret. Paul says these gifts are fine, but without love underneath them, the gifts mean nothing. His description of love (patient, kind, not jealous, not pompous, and so forth) captures the feeling humans universally want to have.

At the end of this passage, Paul contrasts the present world with the one to come. He says now we know partially, but a day will come when we know perfection. We see indistinctly now, Paul says, but one day we shall see face to face. Faith, hope and love remain, but the greatest of these virtues is love.

Many couples see in this passage a description of the love they have for each other, but Paul is encouraging them to have this love for everyone. When you read this passage, try not to think of husband and wife. Think of the people you go to church with. If you love your community this way, you are experiencing God's greatest gift.

Although nearly every couple in love think this passage is ideal for their wedding, it better suits the bride and groom who think of love in terms much bigger than what they experience as partners. Paul is calling us to be loving toward many other people, not just for one other person. This passage is for the bride and groom who love each other, love each other's families, love their co-workers, and love the people who live in their apartment buildings or on their streets. It is for the couple committed to share the eucharist every week with a community of Christians and who love the people who gather there, whether they are close friends or complete strangers. That is the bride and groom who have truly experienced the ideal of love Paul talks about in this famous passage.

[110b]. Ephesians 4, 1–6

Brothers and sisters:
I, a prisoner for the Lord,
   urge you to live in a manner worthy of the call you have received,
   with all humility and gentleness, with patience,
   bearing with one another through love,
   striving to preserve the unity of the spirit
   through the bond of peace:
   one body and one Spirit,
   as you were also called to the one hope of your call;
   one Lord, one faith, one baptism;
   one God and Father of all,
   who is over all and through all and in all.

Preserve unity: one body, one Spirit.

(Note: This passage does not appear in the lectionary's ritual Masses for marriage, but it is included in the second edition of the *Rite of Marriage*. It can be found in the lectionary for Sundays at 110b.)

Many of the New Testament letters have two parts. The first part teaches and the second part exhorts. The second part of these letters often includes an appeal to unity. The early Christian church suffered its times of trials and needed reminders to stay centered on Christ and to support one another. The Letter to the Ephesians fits this pattern.

The author has already reminded the readers of the call they have received. Now the letter urges the Christian community to live with humility and gentleness, bearing with one another through love and striving to preserve unity. There is one body, one Spirit, one hope, one Lord, one faith, one baptism, and there is one God of all, over all, through all, and in all. The loving Christian community experiences the unity that participates in the very life of God.

When this passage is proclaimed at a wedding, it helps the community reflect on the theme of unity. The couple will become one body in their emotional, sexual, and residential life. But this is more than a practical or amorous unity. It is a unity of Christians founded in their union with God and in God's own unique oneness.

> This passage makes a good choice for the bride and groom focused on their own unity, committed to their union with God and the Church, and intent on living and serving in unity. This passage works for those taking seriously their baptismal call to live in humility and patience, bearing with each other in love, and applying those attitudes toward everyone they meet.

6a. * Ephesians 5:2a,21–33 (long form)

Brothers and sisters:
Live in love, as Christ loved us
    and handed himself over for us.

Be subordinate to one another out of reverence for Christ.
Wives should be subordinate to their husbands as to the Lord.
For the husband is head of his wife
    just as Christ is head of the Church,
    he himself the savior of the body.
As the Church is subordinate to Christ,
    so wives should be subordinate to their husbands in everything.
Husbands, love your wives,
    even as Christ loved the Church
    and handed himself over for her to sanctify her,
    cleansing her by the bath of water with the word,
    that he might present to himself the Church in splendor,
    without spot or wrinkle or any such thing,
    that she might be holy and without blemish.

So also husbands should love their wives as their own bodies.
He who loves his wife loves himself.
For no one hates his own flesh
   but rather nourishes and cherishes it,
   even as Christ does the Church,
   because we are members of his Body.

   For this reason a man shall leave his father and his mother
      and be joined to his wife,
   and the two shall become one flesh.

This is a great mystery,
   but I speak in reference to Christ and the Church.
In any case, each one of you should love his wife as himself,
   and the wife should respect her husband.

6b. * Ephesians 2a,5:25–32 (short form)

Brothers and sisters:
Live in love, as Christ loved us
   and handed himself over for us.

Husbands, love your wives,
   even as Christ loved the Church
   and handed himself over for her to sanctify her,
   cleansing her by the bath of water with the word,
   that he might present to himself the Church in splendor,
   without spot or wrinkle or any such thing,
   that she might be holy and without blemish.
So also husbands should love their wives as their own bodies.
He who loves his wife loves himself.
For no one hates his own flesh
   but rather nourishes and cherishes it,
   even as Christ does the Church,
   because we are members of his Body.

   For this reason a man shall leave his father and his mother
      and be joined to his wife,
   and the two shall become one flesh.

This is a great mystery,
    but I speak in reference to Christ and the Church.

The mystery of Christ and the church is like the marriage of husband and wife.

Near the end of the Letter to the Ephesians, the author compares the love of husband and wife to the love of Christ and the church. Many couples will discard the longer form of this reading because of its opening volley, "Wives should be subordinate to their husbands."

This passage begins with a request for the entire Christian community: Live in love, as Christ loved and handed himself over for us. Everyone should follow the example of Christ's love for all people. In the opening lines of this passage, the author describes the kind of love each of us should have toward all, not just toward a spouse.

But then the letter makes an explicit comparison to love in marriage. The longer form of the reading contains the much-maligned passage about the subordination of wives. Although some Christians adhere to this request literally, the Catholic interpretation does not require it. The point of these verses is to show that Christ is head of the church, but by drawing an example from married life, the first-century author has derailed the argument for many people in later cultures. No one argues that Christ is head of the church. But plenty of people argue that the husband is head of his wife.

The command for women to "be subordinate" also poses problems for women with low self-esteem or who find themselves in abusive relationships. This passage provides no justification for making women endure a harmful relationship.

After several verses addressing wives, the author turns to husbands. Here, the request is more relevant. Husbands should love their wives in the way that Christ gave himself up completely for the Church. The self-offering of Christ has purified the church, and the husband's commitment will bring honor to the wife. Just as husbands love their own bodies, so they should also love their wives.

This comparison reaches its climax in the final verse of the reading. "This is a great mystery." The Latin language translates the word "mystery" as "sacramentum." It is from this word that we get our English word "sacrament." This reading is one of the reasons why the Catholic Church lists marriage among our seven sacraments. The New Testament actually calls it one.

This reading is foundational for understanding what the Catholic Church means by the sacrament of marriage. To enter into marriage is to become a sacrament, a sign of the love between Christ and the church. Just as Christ's love is permanent, faithful, and fruitful (giving birth to new members), so also is Christian married love permanent, faithful, and fruitful (giving birth to children). The couple's love brings the love of Christ into the community.

This reading underlies many of the prayers in the marriage rite. The prefaces, blessings, and other prayers recited by the presider make frequent allusions to the sacramental nature of marriage. It is an important reading, and perhaps it is too easily dismissed by many an engaged couple.

> This passage, especially in its longer form, will not make a good choice for a couple focusing on equal roles in marriage. But for the bride and groom intending to love one another with self-sacrifice in a real covenant and not by contract, for those seeing the parallels between their love for each other and Christ's love for the Church, this is an exceptional passage for Christian marriage.

7. Philippians 4:4–9

Brothers and sisters:
Rejoice in the Lord always.
I shall say it again: rejoice!
Your kindness should be known to all.
The Lord is near.
Have no anxiety at all, but in everything,
    by prayer and petition, with thanksgiving,
    make your requests known to God.
Then the peace of God that surpasses all understanding
    will guard your hearts and minds in Christ Jesus.

Finally, brothers and sisters,
    whatever is true, whatever is honorable,
    whatever is just, whatever is pure,
    whatever is lovely, whatever is gracious,
    if there is any excellence
    and if there is anything worthy of praise,
    think about these things.

Keep on doing what you have learned and received
   and heard and seen in me.
Then the God of peace will be with you.

All should know your kindness.

Paul loved his friendship with the Philippians. This letter exudes the warmth of their relationship. Near the end of the epistle, Paul wishes happiness for the community while they await the coming of God. Rejoice, he says, and let everyone see your kindness.

Paul promises that the Lord is near. He tries to calm the anxieties of his friends by encouraging them to pray and to experience the peace of God that surpasses all understanding. If they think about praiseworthy things—whatever is true, honorable, just, pure, lovely, gracious, or excellent—the God of peace will be with them.

This passage was written for a Christian community, not for a married couple. But the parallels are plain. If a married couple lives in the idealized portrait of community life painted by Paul, they, too, can experience the God of peace. The home is the original church. If the bride and groom create a foundational unit of Christianity in their home, they will join with other homes in building a solid Christian community.

> This passage will be a good choice for a couple intending to create a peaceful home with God's help. It is for the couple rejoicing in God's kindness and believing in Christ's coming again. It is for the optimistic bride and groom who harbor happy thoughts of what is praiseworthy.

8. Colossians 3:12–17

Brothers and sisters:
Put on, as God's chosen ones, holy and beloved,
   heartfelt compassion, kindness, humility, gentleness, and
     patience,
   bearing with one another and forgiving one another,
   if one has a grievance against another;
   as the Lord has forgiven you, so must you also do.
And over all these put on love,
   that is, the bond of perfection.

And let the peace of Christ control your hearts,
    the peace into which you were also called in one Body.
And be thankful.
Let the word of Christ dwell in you richly,
    as in all wisdom you teach and admonish one another,
    singing psalms, hymns, and spiritual songs
    with gratitude in your hearts to God.
And whatever you do, in word or in deed,
    do everything in the name of the Lord Jesus,
    giving thanks to God the Father through him.

Wear love over all the other virtues you put on.

The Letter to the Colossians reaches a poetic moment when the author tells the readers to imagine virtues as if they were articles of clothing. Christians should put on compassion, kindness, humility, gentleness, and patience as if they were layering on clothing on a cold day. But over all of these, the writer says, put on love.

Christians should also let the peace of Christ control their hearts and let the word of Christ dwell inside them. Do everything, the letter says, in the name of the LORD Jesus.

In this lovely passage the people are urged to have the right Christian attitude in all they do. They have many virtues, but love should hold them all together.

This passage was written to an entire Christian community, but it appears in the wedding lectionary because it should inspire Christian family life as well. The married couple should live with compassion, kindness, and humility. They should let the word of Christ dwell within their home, and they should do everything in the name of the LORD Jesus.

> If the bride and groom have made Christ the center of their lives, if they reflect on the Scriptures, if they seek peace, if they possess many admirable virtues that foster community life, and if they wear love over everything else, this passage makes a fine choice for a wedding. It will also work if the couple wishes these things for the wedding guests.

9. Hebrews 13:1–4a,5–6b

Brothers and sisters:
Let mutual love continue.
Do not neglect hospitality,
    for through it some have unknowingly
        entertained angels.
Be mindful of prisoners as if sharing their imprisonment,
    and of the ill-treated as of yourselves,
    for you also are in the body.
Let marriage be honored among all
    and the marriage bed be kept undefiled.
Let your life be free from love of money
    but be content with what you have,
    for he has said, *I will never forsake you or abandon you.*
Thus we may say with confidence:

> *The Lord is my helper,*
> *and I will not be afraid.*

Let mutual love continue.

This passage exhorts the Christian community to demonstrate love through hospitality to strangers and through empathy with those in prison and suffering torture. It explicitly calls for faithfulness in marriage and cautions people about greed.

The Letter to the Hebrews closes in the way many other New Testament books do: with an exhortation to the community. This book was written for a group to hear, and its advice concerns group behavior. The passage recommended for weddings opens the final chapter of the book. It is appropriate because of its direct reference to marital faithfulness, but also because of its picture of community life.

If the bride and groom's families are spending a lot of money on the wedding, this reading is going to sound hypocritical when it urges people to be free from the love of money. If the engaged couple is focused more on themselves than on others, or if they give no thought to the suffering, starving, and imprisoned of the world, the same problem appears.

But if the bride and groom have a social conscience evident by the way they share what they own with others, advocate for the oppressed, and desire to do charity more than to receive comfort, they may consider this beautiful text about the Christian life.

10. *1 Peter 3:1–9

Beloved:
You wives should be subordinate to your husbands so that,
    even if some disobey the word,
        they may be won over without a word by their wives' conduct
    when they observe your reverent and chaste behavior.
Your adornment should not be an external one:
    braiding the hair, wearing gold jewelry, or dressing in fine clothes,
    but rather the hidden character of the heart,
    expressed in the imperishable beauty
    of a gentle and calm disposition,
    which is precious in the sight of God.
For this is also how the holy women who hoped in God
    once used to adorn themselves
    and were subordinate to their husbands;
        thus Sarah obeyed Abraham, calling him "lord."
You are her children when you do what is good
    and fear no intimidation.

Likewise, you husbands should live with your wives in
        understanding,
    showing honor to the weaker female sex,
    since we are joint heirs of the gift of life,
    so that your prayers may not be hindered.

Finally, all of you, be of one mind, sympathetic,
    loving toward one another, compassionate, humble.
Do not return evil for evil, or insult for insult;
    but, on the contrary, a blessing, because to this you were called,
    that you might inherit a blessing.

Husbands and wives should be considerate of each other.

This passage will be widely ignored by engaged couples because it seems sexist to many cultures.

The exhortation unfolds in three parts: It is first addressed to wives, then to husbands, and then to the entire community. Wives are asked to accept the authority of their husbands, to not braid their hair, and to not wear gold jewelry or expensive clothes. Their true beauty should come from within, a gentle and quiet spirit.

Husbands are asked to honor their wives as the weaker sex. The wives among the Christian faithful will inherit eternal life just as Christian husbands will. When husbands honor their wives, the letter argues, nothing will hinder their prayers. Consideration in the home has a spiritual goal: It helps the household pray.

Finally, this passage encourages all members of the Christian community to have unity, sympathy, love, and humility. When evil comes their way or they are abused by their enemies, members of the community should repay with a blessing.

> It is easy to see why so many couples reject this passage. It calls for wives to quietly obey husbands and to avoid the trappings of exterior beauty that are so appealing, especially on a wedding day. But the passage conceals some challenging messages for the bride and groom open enough to hear them: Beauty comes from within, not by external adornment. Simplicity of lifestyle is countercultural, but it alerts friends and family to the significance of inner virtue over showy exteriors. Husbands and wives should mutually support each other. Prayer should be a goal for their home life. The bride and groom should take their place within the broader Christian community in a spirit of sympathy and humility. If those values speak to the couple, this might be a good passage to consider for the wedding.

11. 1 John 3:18–24

> Children, let us love not in word or speech
>   but in deed and truth.
>
> Now this is how we shall know that we belong to the truth
>   and reassure our hearts before him
>   in whatever our hearts condemn,
>   for God is greater than our hearts and knows everything.

Beloved, if our hearts do not condemn us,
  we have confidence in God
  and receive from him whatever we ask,
  because we keep his commandments and do what pleases him.
And his commandment is this:
  we should believe in the name of his Son, Jesus Christ,
  and love one another just as he commanded us.
Those who keep his commandments remain in him, and he in
      them,
  and the way we know that he remains in us
  is from the Spirit that he gave us.

Let us love in deed and truth.

This passage asks a Christian community to live sincerely. Love is at the heart of the Christian life; yet some people say they love, but do not act on it. Their love is false. If we love sincerely by acting on our words, we will please God and receive whatever we ask in prayer.

The letter also says that God has commanded us to believe in the name of Jesus Christ and to love one another. The Spirit helps us know when we have kept God's commands.

Although these verses do not explicitly refer to marriage, they do underscore the centrality of love in the Christian life. They also stress that love must be sincere. Those who say they have love should act on it. Otherwise, their love is false. Love is a command from God, and the Spirit will let us know how well we are keeping it.

> This passage will especially work for the bride and groom who give ample demonstrations of love to each other and to the community. If their generosity and charity is notable, it will be clear that they mean the loving words they say. This passage will challenge people to do something about the love they experience.

12. 1 John 4:7–12

Beloved, let us love one another,
  because love is of God;
  everyone who loves is begotten by God and knows God.
Whoever is without love does not know God, for God is love.
In this way the love of God was revealed to us:

God sent his only-begotten Son into the world
    so that we might have life through him.
In this is love:
    not that we have loved God, but that he loved us
    and sent his Son as expiation for our sins.
Beloved, of God so loved us,
    we also must love one another.
No one has ever seen God.
Yet, if we love one another, God remains in us,
    and his love is brought to perfection in us.

God is love.

This beautiful passage reflects deeply on the mystery of love. The love we experience as humans completely fills us. We enjoy the feeling so much we hunger for more. True love will call us into actions of charity toward others.

The First Letter of John argues that love comes first from God. Love is not so much something we fall into, as something that God has given to us. God loved us so much that Jesus the divine Son came for our salvation.

When we love, the letter says, we participate in God. God's love comes to perfection in us when we love others. Therefore, members of the Christian community should express love for one another. In doing so, we not only receive the happiness that comes from human love, but we also experience divine love. Human affection brings divine benefit.

> This passage will work perfectly for the couple having a spiritual experience through their own love. They realize that their love for each other is bigger than they are. It has God as its origin, and it has others as its destiny. Love dwells within us, but passes through us toward others. In that mystery of charity we meet God.

13. Revelation 19:1,5–9a

I, John, heard what sounded like the loud voice
    of a great multitude in heaven, saying:

"Alleluia!
Salvation, glory, and might belong to our God."

A voice coming from the throne said:

"Praise our God, all you his servants,
    and you who revere him, small and great."

Then I heard something like the sound of a great multitude
    or the sound of rushing water or mighty peals of thunder,
    as they said:
    "Alleluia!
    The Lord has established his reign,
        our God, the almighty.
    Let us rejoice and be glad
        and give him glory.
    For the wedding day of the Lamb has come,
        his bride has made herself ready.
    She was allowed to wear
        a bright, clean linen garment."
(The linen represents the righteous deeds of the holy ones.)

Then the angel said to me,
    "Write this:
    Blessed are those who have been called
    to the wedding feast of the Lamb."

Blessed are those called to the wedding feast of the Lamb.

The last book of the Bible is also the most visionary. It unveils the mystery of God and redemption through symbolism.

In this passage, John, the visionary, hears a dialogue between a great multitude in heaven and a voice from the throne, all calling out praise to God. The occasion for this praise is the wedding of the Lamb and his bride. The Lamb represents Christ and the bride represents the church, clothed in the good deeds of the Christian faithful. The angel tells John, "Blessed are those who have been called to the wedding feast of the Lamb."

In the eyes of the church, when any Christian bride and groom marry they become a symbol of the church and Christ. This vision from Revelation is one reason why. It interprets eternal life as the joining

49

together of the Christian faithful with Jesus. The joy of that union can be compared to the happiness of a wedding banquet. A Christian wedding, then, foreshadows a happy eternal life.

> The symbolism of this passage is not easy to grasp in one reading, but it may appeal to couples especially connected with Christ and the church. They will experience in their friendship a sign of God's love. They look forward in hope for a life after death. They know what it is to be joyful in each other's presence, and they desire that kind of joy forever in heaven with Christ.

Responsorial Psalms

The bride and groom may be choosing the responsorial psalm with the help of the wedding musician. Many couples pick this piece because they like the music. But it would be worthwhile first of all to choose the best text.

1. 33:12 and 18,20–21,22

R. (5b) The earth is full of the goodness of the Lord.
Blessed the nation whose God is the LORD,
   the people he has chosen for his own inheritance.
But see, the eyes of the LORD are upon those who fear him,
   upon those who hope for his kindness.
R. The earth is full of the goodness of the Lord.
Our soul waits for the LORD,
   who is our help and our shield,
For in him our hearts rejoice;
   in his holy name we trust.
R. The earth is full of the goodness of the Lord.
May your kindness, O LORD, be upon us
   who have put our hope in you.
R. The earth is full of the goodness of the Lord.

God's kindness fills the earth.

This prayer praises God's goodness. It acknowledges the kindness God shows to the nations chosen for divine inheritance. The psalmist also prays that God will show kindness to all those who hope for it.

This psalm appears in the wedding lectionary for several reasons. Primarily, it stresses kindness, a quality that married couples try to imitate. That kindness typifies the demeanor of the God who entered into a covenant with Israel. The Israelites could not give back to God an equal measure of what God gave them. God's kindness created the covenant. That kindness, which expects not to receive equally in return, should also typify Christian marriage.

This psalm develops other themes pertinent to marriage. God chooses people for a relationship in the way that a couple chooses freely to enter into the bond of marriage. The psalm also prays that God will show kindness to those who hope for it. It should inspire the couple to should show kindness to other people.

> In the complete lectionary, this psalm sometimes follows a first reading about creation because of its refrain about the good earth. It would be especially appropriate if the couple has chosen as their first reading one of the passages from Genesis about the creation of the world or about the covenant. This psalm also fits the wedding of a bride and groom who outdo each other in acts of kindness, and who intend to do the same with their children, the church, and the whole community.

2. 34:2–3,4–5,6–7,8–9

R. (2a) I will bless the Lord at all times.
   or:
R. (9a) Taste and see the goodness of the Lord.
I will bless the LORD at all times;
   his praise shall be ever in my mouth.
Let my soul glory in the LORD;
   the lowly will hear me and be glad.
R. I will bless the Lord at all times.
   or:
R. Taste and see the goodness of the Lord.
Glorify the LORD with me,
   let us together extol his name.
I sought the LORD, and he answered me
   and delivered me from all my fears.
R. I will bless the Lord at all times.
   or:

R. Taste and see the goodness of the Lord.
Look to him that you may be radiant with joy,
    and your faces may not blush with shame.
When the poor one called out, the LORD heard,
    and from all his distress he saved him.
R. I will bless the Lord at all times.
    or:
R. Taste and see the goodness of the Lord.
The angel of the LORD encamps
    around those who fear him, and delivers them.
Taste and see how good the LORD is;
    blessed the man who takes refuge in him.
R. I will bless the Lord at all times.
    or:
R. Taste and see the goodness of the Lord.

Praise God at all times.

Every line of this psalm begins a new thought, but all the verses give
reasons to praise God. The singer praises God at all times. The lowly
rejoice in God's mercy. God delivers us from our fears. God gives us joy.
God saves the afflicted. The faithful can taste and see how good God is.
All these sentiments spill one on top of the other in the verses of this
song of praise.

> This psalm works especially well with passages that speak of God's
> protection or of the vision of the heavenly banquet. It is a good
> choice for the couple rejoicing in God's goodness to them and to
> the community. If the bride and groom want to thank God for all
> that has happened to them, but they cannot find the words to
> say, this psalm may provide what they need.

3. 103:1–2,8 and 13,17–18a

R. (8a) The Lord is kind and merciful.
    or:
R. (see 17) The Lord's kindness is everlasting to those who fear him.
Bless the LORD, O my soul;
    and all my being, bless his holy name.
Bless the LORD, O my soul,

and forget not all his benefits.
R. The Lord is kind and merciful.
   or:
R. The Lord's kindness is everlasting to those who fear him.
Merciful and gracious is the LORD,
   slow to anger and abounding in kindness.
As a father has compassion on his children,
   so the LORD has compassion on those who fear him.
R. The Lord is kind and merciful.
   or:
R. The Lord's kindness is everlasting to those who fear him.
But the kindness of the LORD is from eternity
   to eternity toward those who fear him,
And his justice towards children's children
   among those who keep his covenant.
R. The Lord is kind and merciful.
   or:
R. The Lord's kindness is everlasting to those who fear him.

God is kind and merciful.

This psalm also praises God's mercy. God is slow to anger and rich in kindness. God has compassion on people as parents have compassion for their children. God especially blesses those who keep the covenant.
This psalm celebrates the covenant between God and the chosen people. The people realized that they could not bring to this covenant anything that God did not already have. So the covenant symbolizes God's overwhelming love for those who have not earned it and cannot completely return it. All God asked was faithfulness. This psalm demonstrates that unusual gift of love given not with the expectation of getting something equal in return, but in receiving faithfulness.

> This psalm works very well with a first reading about the covenant because the covenant becomes a model for married love. It is also appropriate for the bride and groom who give to each other without expecting an equal return. It fits committed partners who each think he or she is receiving more than could possibly be given back.

4. 112:1bc–2,3–4,5–7a,7b–8,9

R. (see 1) Blessed the man who greatly delights in the Lord's
    commands.
    or:
R. Alleluia.
Blessed the man who fears the LORD,
    who greatly delights in his commands.
His posterity shall be mighty upon the earth;
    the upright generation shall be blessed.
R. Blessed the man who greatly delights in the Lord's commands.
    or:
R. Alleluia.
Wealth and riches shall be in his house;
    his generosity shall endure forever.
Light shines through the darkness for the upright;
    he is gracious and merciful and just.
R. Blessed the man who greatly delights in the Lord's commands.
    or:
R. Alleluia.
Well for the man who is gracious and lends,
    who conducts his affairs with justice;
He shall never be moved;
    the just one shall be in everlasting remembrance.
An evil report he shall not fear.
R. Blessed the man who greatly delights in the Lord's commands.
    or:
R. Alleluia.
His heart is firm, trusting in the LORD.
His heart is steadfast; he shall not fear
    till he looks down upon his foes.
R. Blessed the man who greatly delights in the Lord's commands.
    or:
R. Alleluia.
Lavishly he gives to the poor;
    his generosity shall endure forever;
    his horn shall be exalted in glory.
R. Blessed the man who greatly delights in the Lord's commands.
    or:
R. Alleluia.

Those who delight in God's commands are blessed.

This psalm tells of the blessings bestowed on those who are faithful to God's commands. They will have mighty descendants. The light will shine bright for them. They need not fear judgment. All this is theirs if they are upright, gracious, merciful, just, honest, steadfast, and charitable to the poor.

This psalm highlights the themes of covenant and charity. The covenant that God established with ancient Israel models the kind of covenant that marriage becomes. Those who are faithful to the covenant receive many blessings. But keeping that covenant demands actions of charity. As the bride and groom begin their life together, they are called to love each other, but also to love the poor and to live in honesty and kindness. The couple with these virtues will experience the blessings God promises the just.

> This psalm works well with a first reading about the covenant or the charitable responsibilities of the Christian community. It will lay out the Christian responsibility to the poor and needy. It will either affirm or challenge the couple and the community.

5. * 128:1–2,3,4–5

R. (see 1a) Blessed are those who fear the Lord.
or:
R. (4) See how the Lord blesses those who fear him.
Blessed are you who fear the LORD,
  who walk in his ways!
For you shall eat the fruit of your handiwork;
  blessed shall you be, and favored.
R. Blessed are those who fear the Lord.
or:
R. See how the Lord blesses those who fear him.
Your wife shall be like a fruitful vine
  in the recesses of your home;
Your children like olive plants
  around your table.
R. Blessed are those who fear the Lord.
or:
R. See how the Lord blesses those who fear him.

Behold thus is the man blessed
 who fears the LORD.
The LORD bless you from Zion:
 may you see the prosperity of Jerusalem
 all the days of your life.
R. Blessed are those who fear the Lord.
 or:
R. See how the Lord blesses those who fear him.

Those who fear God enjoy blessings including the gift of a family.

This psalm praises those who walk in God's ways. Those who are faithful to God will gain favorable results for their work. They will also enjoy a full family life. God will bless them with the gift of children. Their prosperity will signify God's blessing.

When sung at a wedding, this psalm acknowledges those who are faithful to God. It assumes that the bride and groom are among those who seek to please God, and it raises expectations that they will enjoy the blessing of children among their divine rewards. If they live as God has taught, walking in God's ways, they should experience blessings at work, at home, and in the community.

> This psalm pairs well with a reading about the covenant or about one's hopes for family life. It works very well for a bride and groom praying for the gift of children with whom they plan to share their love.

6. 145:8–9,10 and 15,17–18

R. (9a) The Lord is compassionate toward all his works.
The LORD is gracious and merciful,
 slow to anger and of great kindness.
The LORD is good to all
 and compassionate toward all his works.
R. The Lord is compassionate toward all his works.
Let all your works give you thanks, O LORD,
 and let your faithful ones bless you.
The eyes of all look hopefully to you
 and you give them their food in due season.
R. The Lord is compassionate toward all his works.

The LORD is just in all his ways
    and holy in all his works.
The LORD is near to all who call upon him,
    to all who call upon him in truth.
R. The Lord is compassionate toward all his works.

God is kind to all.

This psalm praises God with many descriptions: God is slow to anger, kind, compassionate, provident, just, holy, and near. To such a God, the eyes of all creatures look with hope, and God gives them all they need. God cares for all who pray in truth.

This is the God to whom we turn on a wedding day. We ask God to show these qualities to the couple. The bride and groom turn their eyes to God with hope. They ask God to provide all the things they need for their home. God will care for them if they pray in truth.

> This hymn of praise works for almost any couple. It offers praise to the God of all kindness, in hopes that the newlyweds will experience blessings as they begin their new life. If the bride and groom have faith in God, share some reasonable anxiety about the future, and recognize their dependence on God to make the future secure, this psalm is for them.

7. 148:1–2,3–4,9–10,11–13a,13c–14a

R. (13a) Let us praise the name of the Lord.
    or:
R. Alleluia.
Alleluia.
Praise the LORD from the heavens,
    praise him in the heights;
Praise him, all you his angels,
    praise him, all you his hosts.
R. Let us praise the name of the Lord.
    or:
R. Alleluia.
Praise him, sun and moon;
    praise him, all you shining stars.
Praise him, you highest heavens,

and you waters above the heavens.
R. Let us praise the name of the Lord.
   or:
R. Alleluia.
You mountains and all you hills,
   you fruit trees and all you cedars;
You wild beasts and all tame animals,
   you creeping things and winged fowl.
R. Let us praise the name of the Lord.
   or:
R. Alleluia.
Let the kings of the earth and all peoples,
   the princes and all the judges of the earth,
Young men too, and maidens,
   old men and boys,
Praise the name of the LORD,
   for his name alone is exalted.
R. Let us praise the name of the Lord.
   or:
R. Alleluia.
His majesty is above earth and heaven,
   and he has lifted his horn above the people.
R. Let us praise the name of the Lord.
   or:
R. Alleluia.

Praise God's name.

This hymn of praise salutes the holy name of God. It calls upon earth and heaven to render God praise. Stars, angels, mountains, hills, trees, animals, and birds are all summoned to a grand chorus of praise. The reasons for this praise are that God has provided for faithful people and remains close to them.

On the wedding day, this psalm invites all creation to give God praise. The gathered assembly has a very specific reason for giving praise—the joy God has given the bride and groom. The Creator of all things still takes delight in each one.

The creation motif of this psalm also invites thoughts about the future children of this couple. As father and mother, they will join God in the act of creation, conceiving children who will give praise to the Creator of all.

This psalm would make a nice fit with a first reading about creation. It also supports a bride and groom aware of the presence of God in all of nature and the closeness of God to their hearts. For the couple looking forward to raising children in faith, this psalm makes a good choice.

Gospels

1. Matthew 5:1–12a

When Jesus saw the crowds, he went up the mountain,
   and after he had sat down, his disciples came to him.
He began to teach them, saying:

   "Blessed are the poor in spirit,
      for theirs is the Kingdom of heaven.
   Blessed are they who mourn,
      for they will be comforted.
   Blessed are the meek,
      for they will inherit the land.
   Blessed are they who hunger and thirst for righteousness,
      for they will be satisfied.
   Blessed are the merciful,
      for they will be shown mercy.
   Blessed are the clean of heart,
      for they will see God.
   Blessed are the peacemakers,
      for they will be called children of God.
   Blessed are they who are persecuted for the sake of righteousness,
      for theirs is the Kingdom of heaven.
   Blessed are you when they insult you and persecute you
      and utter every kind of evil against you falsely because of me.
   Rejoice and be glad,
      for your reward will be great in heaven."

The reward of the blessed will be great in heaven.

The Beatitudes open the Sermon on the Mount in Matthew's Gospel. Jesus' teaching ministry begins with these words. In them he lays out his charter for human behavior and his assurance of divine reward.

This Gospel appears frequently in the lectionary, including All Saints Day and as one of the options for funerals. It summarizes much of how Jesus expects a good disciple to behave.

At a wedding, the Beatitudes raise some expectations of the couple. As they enter this unique relationship with each other, with the church, and with God, the bride and groom hear Jesus' expectations and promises.

Jesus blesses those who are poor in spirit, who mourn, who are meek, who hunger for righteousness, and who are merciful, clean of heart, and peacemakers. He promises them comfort, inheritance, satisfaction, and a share in the kingdom of heaven.

These words help correct some of the secular notions about marriage. Some couples assume they will be blessed if the wedding shows they are rich in resources, happy, independent, able to hold their own ground, and able to express themselves. The Beatitudes of Jesus have another vision. They praise the virtues of charity and justice.

> This passage makes an especially appropriate choice for those who do not want their wedding to be a mere show but rather a celebration of faith and a challenge to help the needy. This reading will please the bride and groom who have made a commitment to make the world a better place by sharing their love with those in need.

2. Matthew 5:13–16

Jesus said to his disciples:
"You are the salt of the earth.
But if salt loses its taste, with what can it be seasoned?
It is no longer good for anything
    but to be thrown out and trampled underfoot.
You are the light of the world.
A city set on a mountain cannot be hidden.
Nor do they light a lamp and then put it under a bushel basket;
    it is set on a lamp stand,
    where it gives light to all in the house.
Just so, your light must shine before others,
    that they may see your good deeds
    and glorify your heavenly Father."

You are the light of the world.

Early in his public ministry, while delivering his Sermon on the Mount, Jesus compares good disciples to salt and light. A little bit of salt seasons food. But if the salt is bad it is good for nothing. Light has its effect when it is lifted high, not placed under a basket. If everyone can see the good deeds of the disciples, their small efforts will shine far and wide.

At this point in the Gospel story, Jesus has been gathering his first disciples. He wants to form them now as his messengers. He teaches them the wisdom that has shaped his heart, that will direct their lives, and that they will pass on to others. When they accept this teaching and live by it, they will set an example for the entire world to see.

This passage appears in the wedding lectionary to remind the couple and the community to be good examples as disciples of Jesus. When the church celebrates marriage, we celebrate the forming of a new Christian household, a place where disciples dwell. This new household resembles the community of new disciples to whom Jesus addressed these words.

The couple shares a call to be salt and light for the world. As a community, we expect this couple to live in a way that will impress others by a love for Christ and service to others. Their good deeds will shine a light that will cause others to praise God.

> This passage makes a good choice for a couple with a strong faith in God and who put that faith into action. If the bride and groom can give examples of how they serve the community and share the message of the Gospel, this passage will ring true.

3a. Matthew 7:21, 24–29 (long form)

Jesus said to his disciples:
"Not everyone who says to me, 'Lord, Lord,'
    will enter the Kingdom of heaven,
    but only the one who does the will of my Father in heaven.

"Everyone who listens to these words of mine and acts on them
    will be like a wise man who built his house on rock.
The rain fell, the floods came,
    and the winds blew and buffeted the house.

But it did not collapse;
    it had been set solidly on rock.
And everyone who listens to these words of mine
    but does not act on them
    will be like a fool who built his house on sand.
The rain fell, the floods came,
    and the winds blew and buffeted the house.
And it collapsed and was completely ruined."

When Jesus finished these words,
    the crowds were astonished at his teaching,
    for he taught them as one having authority,
    and not as their scribes.

3b. Matthew 7:21,24–25 (short form)

Jesus said to his disciples:
"Not everyone who says to me, 'Lord, Lord,'
    will enter the Kingdom of heaven,
    but only the one who does the will of my Father in heaven.

"Everyone who listens to these words of mine and acts on them
    will be like a wise man who built his house on rock.
The rain fell, the floods came,
    and the winds blew and buffeted the house.
But it did not collapse;
    it had been set solidly on rock."

The house built on rock will not collapse.

Jesus compares good disciples to those who build their home on a solid foundation. A well-built house will not collapse in a storm. But the fool who builds a house on sand will see it fall into ruins. The foundation for discipleship, Jesus says, is his words. Build the foundation of your life on the words of Jesus, and no storm can tear down that house.

This text is another excerpt from the Sermon on the Mount. Throughout this sermon, Jesus shares his wisdom with his new community of disciples. He gives some very practical advice, as well as spiritual direction. If they have the words of Jesus at the core of their beings, they will make good decisions and accomplish great things.

As the newlyweds establish a home for themselves, these words will take on special meaning. They will have many concerns about building a strong foundation literally and figuratively. They will want to live in a physical building that will be safe and secure. But they will also want their relationship to start strong. Their love for each other and their love for Christ will lay a foundation upon which they can build the strong spiritual structure of a loving home.

> This Gospel will inspire those wishing to make the words of Jesus a foundation for their lives and their home. If the couple is already faithful in prayer and attentive to the words of Christ, this passage will make a good choice. If the bride and groom pray over the decisions they wish to make, if they have ever served as lectors or catechists, if they have concerns about where they plan to live and how to make ends meet, they will find affirmation and comfort in this text.

4. * Matthew 19:3–6

Some Pharisees approached Jesus, and tested him, saying,
"Is it lawful for a man to divorce his wife for any cause whatever?"
He said in reply, "Have you not read that from the beginning
the Creator *made them male and female* and said,
For this reason a man shall leave his father and mother
and be joined to his wife, and the two shall become one flesh?
So they are no longer two, but one flesh.
Therefore, what God has joined together, man must not separate."

Let no one separate what God has joined.

Jesus responds to a question about divorce. The query comes from the Pharisees, a group set at odds with Jesus throughout the Gospel. They do not ask out of idle curiosity. They are asking this to trap Jesus, to see if he will say something illegal. Still, the story provides an opportunity for hearing Jesus' thoughts about marriage. The passage is almost identical to the one from Mark (10:6–9). In Mark the Pharisees ask, "Is it lawful to divorce?" But in Matthew they ask more pointedly,

"Is it lawful to divorce for any cause whatever?" This version of the question appears in the wedding lectionary.

In reply, Jesus retells the Pharisees the story of creation from the Book of Genesis. God created human beings male and female for the purpose of forming a family. A man leaves his parents and takes his own wife so that the two may become one flesh. Jesus says that no one should separate what God has joined.

This Gospel makes a logical choice for a wedding because it contains Jesus' explicit reflections on the purposes of married life. Marriage joins two individuals as one. Marriage begins a new family. Marriage is permanent. Marriage has its roots in God's creation of the world.

This passage is a good choice for a couple focused on these ideals of marriage. The opening question from the Pharisees, however, will cause divorced people at the ceremony to squirm. Sometimes the parents of the bride and groom themselves are divorced, and they will feel discomfort from Jesus' final words: Let no one separate what God has joined.

> If the bride and groom want to underscore their commitment to the permanence of marriage and the raising of children, they may choose this passage for their wedding. If they have experienced the strain that divorce can bring, if they are determined to be faithful for life, if they recognize that their commitment to each other is rooted not just in human love but in a divine call, the bride and groom will find this text most appropriate.

5. Matthew 22:35–40

One of the Pharisees, a scholar of the law, tested Jesus by asking,
　　"Teacher, which commandment in the law is the greatest?"
He said to him,
　　"You shall love the Lord, your God,
　　with all your heart,
　　with all your soul,
　　and with all your mind.
This is the greatest and the first commandment.
The second is like it:
　　You shall love your neighbor as yourself.
The whole law and the prophets depend on these two
　　　　commandments."

Love God and love your neighbor.

At the end of Matthew's Gospel, Jesus has entered the city of Jerusalem to the acclaim of supporters with palm branches, and his death is imminent. He speaks words that are very dear to him, words he hopes the disciples will always remember.

The Pharisees try to trap Jesus with a question: Which commandment in the law is the greatest? Jesus responds eloquently. He quotes a classic text from the Book of Deuteronomy (6:5): You shall love the Lord, your God, with all your heart, soul, and mind. Then he adds another commandment from Leviticus (19:18): You shall love your neighbor as yourself. One of Jesus' greatest contributions to the history of spirituality was to link these two biblical quotes. They form a quick summary of the divine law for those who wish to follow Christ.

Significantly, this conversation takes place at the end of Jesus' life. As his own life reaches its climax he summarizes his teaching in memorable form. Jesus is about to show the depth of his love by offering his life for his friends.

This beautiful passage naturally fits a wedding. As we gather for the celebration of a very personal human love, we hear of its context in divine love. The first two commandments both have the same purpose as the wedding does: love.

> This passage is especially appropriate for the bride and groom committed to showing their love for God and who demonstrate a love for their neighbors that reaches far beyond care for the future spouse. If they are ready to give their lives for their partner, if their love is as strong as death, the bride and groom will find strength from these words spoken by Jesus as he prepared to lay down his own life for those he loved.

6. * Mark 10:6–9

Jesus said:
"From the beginning of creation,
  God made them male and female.
For this reason a man shall leave his father and mother
  and be joined to his wife,
  and the two shall become one flesh.
So they are no longer two but one flesh.

Therefore what God has joined together,
no human being must separate."

They are no longer two but one flesh.

Both Mark and Matthew report this story in which Jesus takes a
strong position about the permanence of marriage. Although the
Pharisees are not mentioned in this excerpt from Mark, the preceding
verses say they provoke this response with a trick question about
divorce.

Jesus' teaching about marriage is strong and sure. From the
beginning of creation, God created males and females so that two could
become one. The joining of two presumes that their parents will be left
behind. Although Jesus expresses this in terms of the man leaving his
parents behind, the same was and is obviously true of the woman.

Jesus concludes this reflection with a passionate statement: No
human being must separate what God has joined together. This line
will be referenced after the bride and groom exchange their consent in
the ceremony: Let no one separate what God joins.

> The couple wishing to emphasize the seriousness of their
> commitment may find this Gospel attractive. This passage shows
> how Jesus links marriage to God's creation, while underscoring its
> purposes of unity and permanence. If the bride and groom
> appreciate the significance of leaving their homes to start a new
> family and if they are firmly committed to avoid divorce, this text
> will speak to them.

7. * John 2:1–11

There was a wedding in Cana in Galilee,
and the mother of Jesus was there.
Jesus and his disciples were also invited to the wedding.
When the wine ran short,
the mother of Jesus said to him,
"They have no wine."
And Jesus said to her,
"Woman, how does your concern affect me?
My hour has not yet come."
His mother said to the servers,

"Do whatever he tells you."
Now there were six stone water jars there for Jewish ceremonial
    washings,
    each holding twenty to thirty gallons.
Jesus told them,
    "Fill the jars with water."
So they filled them to the brim.
Then he told them,
    "Draw some out now and take it to the headwaiter."
So they took it.
And when the headwaiter tasted the water that had become wine,
    without knowing where it came from
    (although the servants who had drawn the water knew),
    the headwaiter called the bridegroom and said to him,
    "Everyone serves good wine first,
    and then when people have drunk freely, an inferior one;
    but you have kept the good wine until now."
Jesus did this as the beginning of his signs in Cana in Galilee
    and so revealed his glory,
    and his disciples began to believe in him.

Jesus turns water into wine at a wedding in Cana.

Jesus, his disciples, and his mother all attend a wedding at Cana in
Galilee. When the hosts run short of wine, Jesus' mother prompts him
to do something about it. Jesus commands the servers to fill six large
jars with water. When they take it to the headwaiter, the water has
become a fine wine. This is the first of Jesus' miracles recorded in
John's Gospel. In performing it, Jesus revealed his glory and his
disciples began to believe in him.

Because this miracle takes place at a wedding banquet, and because
it reveals Jesus' glory, it offers a glimpse of heaven. In another passage
from the school of John, the Book of Revelation compares the final
glory of God to the wedding feast for the Lamb (Jesus Christ) and the
church. The wedding at Cana foreshadows the joy and glory of the
world to come.

On a more earthly level, the story also reflects the care that Jesus
gives to a new family on the wedding day. He pours out his love for
them as fully as the servers who fill the stone water jars to the brim.
His presence transforms family life as thoroughly as he transformed
water into wine. The presence of Jesus in Christian marriage makes the

union a sacrament, a sign of God's love for the church. Marriage is a celebration of Jesus' care for the couple, embraced in a love that is permanent, faithful, true, and fruitful.

> This Gospel will please those who live with their eyes fixed on the world to come, those who hope in eternal life and who believe in the miraculous power of Christ. This passage celebrates the care God gives individual families. It will especially fit the couple aware of the divine presence transforming their thoughts and actions into the words and deeds of Christ. If the bride and groom have had experiences that revealed how much they need God, if they have contemplated death and the promise of the "wedding feast" of eternal life, if they help out those who have less, they will find this Gospel most appropriate for their wedding.

8. John 15: 9–12

Jesus said to his disciples:
"As the Father loves me, so I also love you.
Remain in my love.
If you keep my commandments, you will remain in my love,
     just as I have kept my Father's commandments
     and remain in his love.

"I have told you this so that my joy might be in you
     and your joy might be complete.
This is my commandment: love one another as I love you."

"Remain in my love."

Jesus tells his disciples he loves them, and he asks them to remain in his love by keeping his commandments. If they love one another as he has loved them, their joy will be complete.

These simple words come at the very end of Jesus' life in John's Gospel. Jesus sits with his disciples at table at the Last Supper, and he gives them his final discourse. In speaking his last words to them—words he knows they will remember—Jesus gives the heart of his teaching. He assures them he loves them and he asks them to love others.

Jesus directs these words to his own disciples, but he speaks through them to all who will follow him. Throughout every generation, Christians have felt the assurance of God's love for them and have answered the summons to love others.

At a wedding, the last words of Jesus become very personal again. The bride and groom will feel the warmth of these words as if Jesus were speaking to them: "As the Father loves me, so I also love you." But they will also hear his challenge to love one another.

Most couples are eager to answer this challenge in love for the new spouse. But Jesus has something more in mind—a love that will extend throughout the Christian community.

> The bride and groom whose love for each other moves them to love family, community, and strangers will find this a welcome text on their wedding day. If the bride and groom love as if their life depended on it, if they are ready they encounter, this passage makes a good fit for their wedding.
>
> This text appears in the lectionary for several Masses in the Easter season. If the wedding takes place at that time of year, this passage would be especially appropriate.

9. John 15:12–16

Jesus said to his disciples:
"This is my commandment: love one another as I love you.
No one has greater love than this,
    to lay down one's life for one's friends.
You are my friends if you do what I command you.
I no longer call you slaves,
    because a slave does not know what his master is doing.
I have called you friends,
    because I have told you everything I have heard from my Father.
It was not you who chose me, but I who chose you
    and appointed you to go and bear fruit that will remain,
    so that whatever you ask the Father in my name he may give
      you."

"Love one another as I have loved you."

Jesus asks his disciples to show for each other the same love he shows them. He asks a lot. He lays down his life for the friends he loves. He treats others as friends, not as slaves. He has chosen disciples to go forth and to bear fruit that will endure. But it all depends on his foundational command, love.

This passage comes from the words Jesus addresses to the apostles at the Last Supper. To fully appreciate its significance, imagine Jesus speaking at table on the night before he died. This is his last chance to say things to the friends he loves. He encourages them to love, but he warns them about what love demands.

Death and slavery may not seem appropriate topics for the Gospel at a wedding Mass, but they show how radical is Jesus' call to love. When hearing this passage at a wedding, the bride and groom are reminded that they are to love deep enough to die for their partner. They are to love as true friends, and not take advantage of a spouse as if she or he were a slave.

This passage also reveals the mystery of God's choice. Jesus tells the disciples they did not choose him, but he chose them. In a mysterious way, Christ has chosen the bride and groom to love each other and to live as his disciples. He commands them to go forth and bear fruit that will endure. That fruit will include the children they raise as disciples of the faith, who will share the joy of this day and the mission of Jesus with the world.

> The bride and groom might choose this Gospel if their love really is as strong as death, if they have discussed the worst scenarios with each other, if they do not take advantage of the other's love but let their partner live in freedom. If they understand that God has chosen them and loved them before they have loved each other, and if they desire to return their appreciation to God as a couple by sharing their love in specific ways with the community, they will find this a fine text for their wedding.
>
> If the wedding takes place in the Easter season, this text is especially appropriate. It appears in the lectionary for Sundays and weekdays at that time of year.

10a. John 17:20–26 (long form)

Jesus raised his eyes to heaven and said:
"I pray not only for my disciples,
    but also for those who will believe in me through their word,
    so that they may all be one,
    as you, Father, are in me and I in you,
    that they also may be in us,
    that the world may believe that you sent me.
And I have given them the glory you gave me,
    so that they may be one, as we are one,
    I in them and you in me,
    that they may be brought to perfection as one,
    that the world may know that you sent me,
    and that you loved them even as you loved me.
Father, they are your gift to me.
I wish that where I am they also may be with me,
    that they may see my glory that you gave me,
    because you loved me before the foundation of the world.
Righteous Father, the world also does not know you,
    but I know you, and they know that you sent me.
I made known to them your name and I will make it known,
    that the love with which you loved me
    may be in them and I in them."

10b. John 17:20–23 (short form)

Jesus raised his eyes to heaven and said:
"Holy Father, I pray not only for these,
    but also for those who will believe in me through their word,
    so that they may all be one,
    as you, Father, are in me and I in you,
    that they also may be in us,
    that the world may believe that you sent me.
And I have given them the glory you gave me,
    so that they may be one, as we are one,
    I in them and you in me,
    that they may be brought to perfection as one,
    that the world may know that you sent me,
    and that you loved them even as you loved me."

Jesus prays that all may be one.

At the Last Supper, having finished his final discourse to his disciples, Jesus lifts his eyes to heaven and prays to God on the night before his death.

Jesus prays for the disciples and for those who will believe through their word. He prays that all may be one as he and the Father are one. He has given them the glory that the Father gave him. In this way, the world may know that the Father loves the disciples as the Father loves Jesus. Jesus longs to have his disciples with him in his glory. But while they are in the world, he prays that the Father's love may be in them, and that Jesus himself may be in them.

At a wedding, Jesus' final prayer for love and unity reminds the couple and those in attendance of his hopes for the future of his disciples. The bride and groom are giving a beautiful testimony of love and unity in their lives. This passage reminds family and friends that Christ wishes the same for all of them too. Jesus desired this unity so strongly that it became the content of his final prayer to the Father at the Last Supper the night before he died.

> This passage is especially poignant in weddings when Christians from different faith traditions marry. It reminds us all that Jesus intended the unity of his followers. For the couple celebrating their unanimity in thought, belief, and action, this passage may make a good choice. It will also fit situations where families have experienced division and are striving for unity.
>
> If the wedding takes place during the Easter season, this text makes a good choice because it appears in the lectionary for Mass at the same time.

Homily Worksheet

Before completing this worksheet, review the notes you made to the
questions on pages 5–9.

As the first reading for the wedding, we choose this text:
_____.

- It affirms the couple in this way:

- It challenges the couple in this way:

- It affirms the assembly in this way:

- It challenges the assembly in this way:

As the psalm for the wedding, we choose this text:
_____.

- It affirms the couple in this way:

- It challenges the couple in this way:

- It affirms the assembly in this way:

- It challenges the assembly in this way:

(Optional) As the second reading for the wedding, we choose this text: _____.

- It affirms the couple in this way:

- It challenges the couple in this way:

- It affirms the assembly in this way:

- It challenges the assembly in this way:

As the Gospel for the wedding, we choose this text: _____.

- It affirms the couple in this way:

- It challenges the couple in this way:

- It affirms the assembly in this way:

- It challenges the assembly in this way:

In summary, here are some points we think the homily should make:

These lines of the Scriptures can illustrate those points:

These experiences of the couple can illustrate those points:

Sample Homily

The following example is the homily I gave at my niece's wedding. I had a double role here, of course, as priest and uncle, which shaped how I wrote the talk. I offer it as one example. Obviously, this exact homily will not work at somebody else's wedding. I offer it to you so you can see some of the things to think about. I've included some annotations to help you understand why I wrote the homily this way.

The first time Ben asked Julie for a date, she said no.[1] Well, this happened after the first time, too. Last night people couldn't agree whether Julie said no ten times or twenty times. The rest of the family, though, took a liking to Ben right away. The Turners are grateful that a family as gracious as the Keeches would open their arms to the likes of us.[2]

---

[1] I like to start a wedding homily with some story about the couple. It should not embarrass them. It needs to be honest and true. I find that stories about how the couple met or how the proposal went work very well here. But I try to avoid cheap stories. I want the story to go somewhere. I want it to have a point that fits with the main thrust of the homily. You'll note later that I return to this story.

I kept the opening light-hearted. I was not trying for a big laugh, just a smile. It should also be evident from the way the homily is given that the preacher loves the couple. This celebration of love will not feel sincere if the preacher does not join in the loving atmosphere of the wedding. The tone of voice from the first line of the homily should already send a message of affection.

[2] I meant this sincerely. Ben's family is a great bunch of folks. Our family felt honored to be included with them. A lot of times there is some wariness between the families. When there is joyful acceptance, I like to affirm it for everyone.

Actually, Turner family members have worked for causes like social services, battered women, anti-drug abuse, the injured, the county, the city, and the church. Ben and Julie met each other at a workplace dedicated to the cause of a hearty breakfast.[3] They've been dedicated to their education: Ben will soon finish his degree, and Julie has been named Avila college's outstanding graduate in the field of education this year.[4] But they have not let their education get in the way of pursuing interests like softball and golf—not real sports like baseball, but diverting forms of amusement, nonetheless.[5]

One piece of advice they give people in sports applies to much of life as well.[6] Learn the fundamentals. If you do the fundamentals well, good things will happen. If you can throw, catch, hit, hit for power, and run (the five tools of baseball), good things will happen, even without giving it much thought. First Watch seemed like a good place to work—fundamentally a good decision. You don't always know where a decision like that will lead, but if you learn the fundamentals of good decision-making, good things will happen. If you learn the fundamentals of family life, good things will

---

[3] They met each other while working at a local restaurant, First Watch, that specialized in breakfast fare.

[4] Julie got a much deserved round of applause here. The announcement had just been made and not everyone had heard the news. The applause served another function: It gave the assembly something to do together. Whether it's song, laughter, a smile, applause, or just a glow in the heart—I like to find something for all those guests who do not know one another to help them express the united feelings that brought them together for this wedding.

[5] Underneath this is my own love for baseball and Ben's love for golf. Again, I'm trying to establish in a few lines my affection for the couple and my knowledge of their interests. Too frequently at a wedding the preacher seems not to know who the couple is, what they enjoy doing and what their families are like. Part of the marriage preparation can help the preacher explore these areas and to acknowledge them. The subtext is that the whole church cares about this couple as people and that we believe this particular couple has something to offer back to the church.

[6] Both Ben and Julie are sports enthusiasts. Julie was a fine softball catcher and Ben still coaches. That is why I made continued references to the world of sports in this particular wedding homily.

happen. Both of you know that firsthand from the families you have.[7]

St. Paul wanted the early church to learn the fundamentals as well.[8] Christians in Corinth had a lot of problems. They bickered about their leaders. They misbehaved at Eucharist. They didn't share their food with the hungry. It was a mess. Paul said to them, "You gotta get back to fundamentals. And the most fundamental part of being a Christian is love. You must be patient, kind, never rude, not self-seeking. If you learn the fundamental of love, you will not be prone to anger. You will not brood over injuries. Good things will happen."[9] In ancient Corinth, you might say that God asked to date the people, God offered to love them, but the people kept saying no—ten times, twenty times, 3,154 times or more.[10] They kept refusing opportunities for love.

---

[7] Here you can catch my transition from a rule of sports to a rule of life. Ben and Julie had made some good decisions about work and relationship. Those decisions paid off for both of them.

[8] Now comes the transition from rule of life to insight from the church. I'm tracing the theme of fundamentals through all these different aspects.

[9] I'm paraphrasing here, of course. But I wanted to paint a background for my comments on the second reading. They had chosen the famous passage about love from First Corinthians. People hear this passage a lot, but I think they don't know the context very well. Setting the context for it, I hoped to help people hear the passage in a different way.

[10] Here I have referred back to my opening story about Ben wanting to ask Julie out. I am setting their personal story within the broader story of God's love for the church. The number 3,154 was a code between Julie and me. Julie's most favorite baseball player was George Brett, who played for the Royals, our local team in Kansas City. In his career, George got 3,154 hits. That's a statistic that hard-core Brett fans know as well as their own age. For most people at the wedding, that number was just a random number, exaggerated to make a point. But I got the smile from Julie I was hoping for here. My hope was to put her a little more at ease before she and Ben exchanged their consent.

Ben and Julie, you've received a powerful example of love from your parents.[11] You have experienced love for each other like never before. All that love comes first from God, who loved you even before you discovered love. My prayer for you today is that you return the love you receive.[12] Don't refuse the opportunities to share it. May it benefit yourselves, your family, your church, and your community. Love never fails.[13]

---

[11] In discussions prior to the marriage, Ben and Julie told me how proud they were of the example their parents had given them. I wanted to bring that to the fore.

[12] I firmly believe every wedding homily should include some challenge to the couple to live the Christian life more faithfully. Here I'm challenging them to share the love they have received. With some couples, this part of the message could be worded more strongly. It is a reminder that the love they experience with each other should be shared with more than themselves. Many of the Scriptures for a wedding presume this too.

[13] I close with a line from First Corinthians. They really liked this passage from Paul, as many couples do. So I thought this line would make a good close. But I wanted them to hear it differently. In their own experience of love, they think "Love never fails" refers to their love for each other. But in Paul's passage, the sentence means the love within the community will never fail. I wanted them to hear that the love they shared with others would also never fail. There is more love out there to be aware of, to share, and to enjoy.